IF FO(

GREATER THAN A TOURIST BOOK SERIES
REVIEWS FROM READERS

I think the series is wonderful and beneficial for tourists to get information before visiting the city.

-Seckin Zumbul, Izmir Turkey

I am a world traveler who has read many trip guides but this one really made a difference for me. I would call it a heartfelt creation of a local guide expert instead of just a guide.

-Susy, Isla Holbox, Mexico

New to the area like me, this is a must have!

-Joe, Bloomington, USA

This is a good series that gets down to it when looking for things to do at your destination without having to read a novel for just a few ideas.

-Rachel, Monterey, USA

Good information to have to plan my trip to this destination.

-Pennie Farrell, Mexico

Great ideas for a port day.

-Mary Martin USA

Aptly titled, you won't just be a tourist after reading this book. You'll be greater than a tourist!

-Alan Warner, Grand Rapids, USA

Even though I only have three days to spend in San Miguel in an upcoming visit, I will use the author's suggestions to guide some of my time there. An easy read - with chapters named to guide me in directions I want to go.

-Robert Catapano, USA

Great insights from a local perspective! Useful information and a very good value!

-Sarah, USA

This series provides an in-depth experience through the eyes of a local. Reading these series will help you to travel the city in with confidence and it'll make your journey a unique one.

-Andrew Teoh, Ipoh, Malaysia

>TOURIST

GREATER THAN A TOURIST – WEST VIRGINIA USA

50 Travel Tips from a Local

Amanda Wills

Greater Than a Tourist- West Virginia USA Copyright © 2018 by CZYK Publishing LLC. All Rights Reserved.

All rights reserved. No part of this book may be reproduced in any form or by any electronic or mechanical means including information storage and retrieval systems, without permission in writing from the author. The only exception is by a reviewer, who may quote short excerpts in a review.

Cover designed by: Ivana Stamenkovic
Cover Image: https://pixabay.com/en/gazebo-berkeley-spring-west-virginia-

1310852/

Greater Than a Tourist
Visit our website at www.GreaterThanaTourist.com

Lock Haven, PA
All rights reserved.
ISBN: 9781983271229

>TOURIST

>TOURIST
50 TRAVEL TIPS FROM A LOCAL

BOOK DESCRIPTION

Are you excited about planning your next trip?

Do you want to try something new?

Would you like some guidance from a local?

If you answered yes to any of these questions, then this Greater Than a Tourist book is for you.

Greater Than a Tourist- Greater Than a Tourist- West Virginia USA by Amanda Wills offers the inside scoop on West Virginia. Most travel books tell you how to travel like a tourist. Although there is nothing wrong with that, as part of the Greater Than a Tourist series, this book will give you travel tips from someone who has lived at your next travel destination.

In these pages, you will discover advice that will help you throughout your stay. This book will not tell you exact addresses or store hours but instead will give you excitement and knowledge from a local that you may not find in other smaller print travel books.

Travel like a local. Slow down, stay in one place, and get to know the people and the culture. By the time you finish this book, you will be eager and prepared to travel to your next destination.

>TOURIST

TABLE OF CONTENTS

IF FOUND PLEASE RETURN TO:
Greater Than a Tourist Book Series
Reviews from Readers
BOOK DESCRIPTION
TABLE OF CONTENTS
DEDICATION
ABOUT THE AUTHOR
HOW TO USE THIS BOOK
FROM THE PUBLISHER
OUR STORY
WELCOME TO
> TOURIST
INTRODUCTION
1. New River Gorge Bridge: A Sight To See
2. A Good Scare: Lake Shawnee Amusement Park
3. Cass Scenic Railroad
4. Kitschy Wonder In The Mountain State
5. Mothman Mystery
6. Ghost Hunters Paradise
7. Greenbrier Resort
8. Berkeley Springs Castle
9. Beckley Exhibition Coal Mines
10. Hidden Gem And Fun Place To Eat: King Tut
11. Green Bank, WV: Wi-Fi Free

12. Dog Racing In Cross Lanes
13. Hollywood Casino At Charles Town Racing
14. Burning Rock Outdoor Adventure Park
15. Enjoy The Mountains: Snowshoe Mountain Resort
16. Babcock State Park
17. White Water Rafting In New River
18. Secret Sandwich Society
19. Weathered Ground Brewery
20. Tamarack: Crafts, Food, And Fun
21. West Virginia State Fair
22. Via Ferrata
23. Winter Fun At Winterplace
24. Bridge Walk
25. Seneca Rock
26. A True Tree House: Thorny Mountain Fire Tower
27. Summersville Lake
28. Appalachian Trail
29. Lost World Caverns
30. Grandview Outdoor Drama
31. Dolly Sods
33. Swiss Village
34. Harpers Ferry
35. The Coal House
36. Hillbilly Hotdog

>TOURIST

37. Road Kill Cook Off
38. Blackwater Falls State Park
39. US Capitol Building
40. West Virginia State Museum/Cultural Center
41. Heritage Farm Museum and Village
42. Glade Springs Resort
43. Adventures on the Gorge
44. Blueberry Hill
45. Okes Family Farm
46. Charleston, West Virginia
47. Out of the Box Room Escape
48. Lake Stevens
49. Lewisburg Chocolate Festival
50. Harvest Moon And Crafts Festival

TOP REASONS TO BOOK THIS TRIP
50 THINGS TO KNOW ABOUT PACKING LIGHT FOR TRAVEL
Packing and Planning Tips
Travel Questions
Travel Bucket List
NOTES

DEDICATION

This book is dedicated to those who have offered support during the darkest and brightest times and to my mother and grandmother who allowed me to be the country girl that I was meant to be in life. To my grandfather who encouraged having outdoor adventures from creating a fort to playing barefoot in the garden this book is a record of the discoveries made in this wonderful state. This book is also dedicated to those who have helped me along this journey called life, whether you were ahead of me paving the way, supporting me by pushing me forward, or walking beside me as a friend or challenger, you have made this possible.

ABOUT THE AUTHOR

Amanda is a West Virginia native who has lived in a tiny town in southern West Virginia for over thirty years. This born and bred Mountaineer loves to spend time outdoors with her horses or helping to plant the garden. Amanda lives in a log cabin in the woods that overlooks the pasture that is filled with various farm animals that include horses, cattle, goats, and sheep. Formerly a teacher, Amanda now enjoys writing, caring for her animals, and spending time with family and friends. She also takes part in various volunteer activities, church activities, and is a huge Mountaineer fan.

Amanda loves all the seasons of West Virginia and the opportunities each bring. Skiing, swimming, hiking, and attending events large and small are all favorites. Amanda loves to travel and truly enjoys finding both those larger attractions and the small towns that have a hidden gem somewhere within their borders. Join this local in visiting some of the most beautiful and unique areas WV has to offer. Whether you want to shop, take in some local food, or enjoy the outdoors in a variety of ways, this guide will help you find what to do and where to go in West Virginia.

HOW TO USE THIS BOOK

The Greater Than a Tourist book series was written by someone who has lived in an area for over three months. The goal of this book is to help travelers either dream or experience different locations by providing opinions from a local. The author has made suggestions based on their own experiences. Please do your own research before traveling to the area in case the suggested places are unavailable.

FROM THE PUBLISHER

Traveling can be one of the most important parts of a person's life. The anticipation and memories that you have are some of the best. As a publisher of the Greater Than a Tourist book series, as well as the popular 50 Things to Know book series, we strive to help you learn about new places, spark your imagination, and inspire you. Wherever you are and whatever you do I wish you safe, fun, and inspiring travel.

Lisa Rusczyk Ed. D.
CZYK Publishing

OUR STORY

Traveling is a passion of the "Greater than a Tourist" series creator. Lisa studied abroad in college, and for their honeymoon Lisa and her husband toured Europe. During her travels to Malta, an older man tried to give her some advice based on his own experience living on the island since he was a young boy. She was not sure if she should talk to the stranger but was interested in his advice. When traveling to some places she was wary to talk to locals because she was afraid that they weren't being genuine. Through her travels, Lisa learned how much locals had to share with tourists. Lisa created the "Greater Than a Tourist" book series to help connect people with locals. A topic that locals are very passionate about sharing.

>TOURIST

WELCOME TO
> TOURIST

INTRODUCTION

It is not down in any map; true places never are.
—Herman Melville

West Virginia is a state that offers a simplistic natural beauty with a rich historical background. Whether you want to hike in the mountains, view native wildlife, or enjoy top resorts with numerous amenities, this is the state for you. Explore each tip to get experience with many of the interesting stops that can be found in West Virginia. If you are visiting for a day or thinking of moving, West Virginia is like no other place in the world. A modern area that still holds traditional values and a laid back style, West Virginia will always be home for so many.

>TOURIST

1. NEW RIVER GORGE BRIDGE: A SIGHT TO SEE

Few sights in West Virginia are as awe inspiring as the New River Gorge Bridge. One of the largest steel arch bridges of its time, The New River Gorge Bridge not only offers a simpler way to travel, but is home to a large celebration that happens every October. Bridge Day brings travelers from many states and from all over the mountain state. This celebration offers a 5K run, B.A.S.E. jumping, parachuting, rappelling, vendors, a chili cook-off, and live music. A perfect way to experience beautiful views and meet locals while in a family friendly environment, expect to do some walking if attending. If you can attend this event the parachuting is a favorite must watch activity that is only allowed during Bridge Day. If you are trained and want to be part of the parachuting event then you must apply and be approved for this once in a lifetime experience.

2. A GOOD SCARE: LAKE SHAWNEE AMUSEMENT PARK

If visiting West Virginia around Halloween, be prepared for the adventure of a life time at Lake Shawnee Amusement Park. This long forgotten amusement park was built on top of an American Indian burial ground. Built on the site of the Clay family massacre, this amusement park was built to entertain the families of local coal miners. The old rickety steel and wood rides still stand in disarray, but the park officially closed in 1966 after two children were killed on the grounds. Now, haunted tours can be taken through the park around Halloween. The admission fee is low, but the tour requires lots of walking through sometimes miry conditions. Perfect for those that like a good scare around that time of year. Most years an overnight stay can also be arranged. This old park is located just outside of the small town of Kegley, WV. This writer attended for the first time about three years ago and the entire walk gave you the feeling of being watched. I am not sure whether it was a ghost or just my mind but I will go again. Take a tour to see if you spot any lingering spirits.

>TOURIST

3. CASS SCENIC RAILROAD

Adults and children alike will enjoy a relaxed day of fun and learning in Pocahontas county West Virginia. Cass Scenic Railroad State Park, located in Cass, WV, features a beautiful state park with an 11-mile long heritage railroad. Learn about steam engines in the museum, go on a scenic trail ride, and try your hand at geocaching. The park also offers fishing, biking, and hiking areas for visitors. The train ride gives those onboard a look at the beautiful natural scenery in the area, a chance to see wildlife, and to experience riding an old steam engine like those many years ago. Various events are available for park visitors during the summer months, specifics can be found online. This is perfect for children and train enthusiasts, including the winding train ride that allows you to rest, unwind, and enjoy the scenery.

4. KITSCHY WONDER IN THE MOUNTAIN STATE

Small towns truly hide the hidden gems of West Virginia and Ansted is no different. Located in Ansted is a small roadside oddity that should not be ignored. Mystery Hole takes you back to a simpler time when roadside attractions were meant to be fun. Stop by to see water roll uphill and enter a room where no one can seem to stand straight. While Mystery Hole was closed for a while, the same family still runs this carnival-like attraction today. A few years ago this attraction had to close and it was like the ending of an era, luckily, the same family was able to reopen it and the mysteries are still something to look forward to on every visit. Though the tricks and illusions can be explained, knowing the science behind these mind blowing mysteries detracts from the fun. A simple activity that will keep you entertained while visiting the state.

5. MOTHMAN MYSTERY

Growing up every local knew about the Mothman mysteries in Point Pleasant, WV. The creature had a moth-like face, but a human body with large wings and glowing red eyes. The creature appeared randomly around the same area for a year in the mid-sixties. Visit the store front museum to learn the urban legend that spurred books, movies, and fear for years. This local used to read the many stories of the Mothman to her students and they were always favorites. Though it has been awhile since a sighting was reported, the legend remains very well-known with people waiting for the Mothman to reappear.

6. GHOST HUNTERS PARADISE

Though this writer is a bit of a wimp for those who like a good scare West Virginia offers many opportunities. Located in Weston, WV the long closed Trans-Alleghany Lunatic Asylum can spark the interest in the most morbid of individuals. Said to be haunted there have been plenty of past patient sightings at this local attraction. Many say the building is haunted by former patients who were treated horribly, some believe it is past workers that still wander the halls, visit and make your own decisions. If the asylum peaks your interest then stop by the West Virginia State Penitentiary in Moundsville. This now closed prison went beyond the usual blood and gore of a prison to having multiple executions performed there. Many were hangings that were open to the public. The hangings were changed to by invitation only after a hanging led to a man being decapitated and the head falling into the crowd. Visitors report ghosts of past guards and inmates as well as that of Shadow Man that roams the halls at all times. Shadow Man is still a legend that is well-known and respected in the area with people still reporting seeing this shadowy figure many nights. Thought to be either RD Walls, a prisoner who was murdered in the seventies or a prison guard thought to be keeping the prison in check; Shadow Man has been extensively studied and hunted.

7. GREENBRIER RESORT

The Greenbrier located in Greenbrier County, WV is much more than a resort known for its bold prints and expansive rooms. This is also the sight of the Congressional fallout shelter that can be toured at certain times each week. Upscale shopping, food, and golf are center to this resort. There are over twenty restaurants and lounges in the resort and a casino on the grounds. Take a tour and then enjoy a night or a week at this well-known attraction. Perfect as a vacation spot or as a gift for the golf lovers in your life to spend time. Even if you do not golf, this resort will keep guests busy for days exploring all there is to see.

>TOURIST

8. BERKELEY SPRINGS CASTLE

West Virginia has its own castle that is nestled securely in the mountains and overlooking the beautiful landscape that is almost heaven. The castle was originally owned by a wealthy widow that enjoyed the best of the best in this beautiful stone castle. Originally owned by Samuel Taylor Suit who was a successful whiskey distiller who built the castle for his third wife, but died before its completion. For years the wife had lavish parties, but as the memories died out so did her desire to stay. The castle was rented out for a while and then used as a boy's camp. Though it is now privately owned you can rent the space for special events if desired. View the castle on the hill while visiting Berkley Springs a known spa town. The castle can be seen from the road below.

9. BECKLEY EXHIBITION COAL MINES

Experience going underground just as the coal miners at Beckley's historic coal mines during many months of the year. The coal mines do not operate rides in winter months for safety issues. For a nominal fee patrons can ride the automated mini-train through the coal mines to get a glimpse into the history of coal mining. During Halloween a haunted mines is created for those who are not faint of heart. Right next door is a small park and hiking trail as well as a youth museum that offers tours through a one room school house and old farm house. Make a day with your family as you visit the mountain state. As someone who has lived here for years this is still an activity I enjoy. Where else will you get a chance to go underground into a real coal mine?

10. HIDDEN GEM AND FUN PLACE TO EAT: KING TUT

If you are in the area of Beckley, West Virginia stop in for a meal at King Tut Drive In. Simply pull in any day of the week except Wednesday and a friendly waitress will come take your order at this old style drive-in. No menus needed as the entire list of available foods are hand painted on wooden signs on the front of the building. This writer thinks the BBQs on homemade rolls are the best, but many swear by the hot dogs. If you aren't a fan of the WV tradition of coleslaw on your hot dog make sure to let them know. If you can handle dessert after a whole meal take home a piece of pie or a whole one to share. This local recommends the apple, but the choice is all yours. When you are finished your tray will be taken and you can leave with a full feeling and a desire to visit again very soon.

11. GREEN BANK, WV: WI-FI FREE

Feeling the need to get your families to disconnect for a bit? Take a road trip to Green Bank, West Virginia. This small rural town in the eastern panhandle of West Virginia has become a go to spot for those suffering from Electromagnetic Hypersensitivity, those bothered by the electromagnetic fields given off by all our connected devices. While this may not be a place most people would want to live, it is a great place to visit and disconnect from the overly connected world for a few days. It is odd to drive through the area for the first time and suddenly you have no cell phone signal, but for those who need such a place, this is a wonderful little town.

12. DOG RACING IN CROSS LANES

For those that like a little excitement as part of their vacation, Cross Lanes, West Virginia offers the thrill of dog racing and video gaming machines all under one roof. The casino type atmosphere has an attached resort with all the amenities that one would need for a weekend of longer. Play some slots, maybe a round of video poker, bet on telecast horse races, or take a chance on the dogs. Go visit the dogs just before the race to get up close to your future winner. Watch the races on the screen from a table, through the large glass at the track, or stand outside and root for your canine to run as fast as possible. Take a break from gaming to enjoy one of many food choices in the gaming area. This is a great place to unwind and relax. If you want to stay up all night gambling the rooms have a late check out so you can sleep in if needed. Children are allowed on the lower deck to watch the dog races, but not on the upper deck where video gambling occurs.

>TOURIST

13. HOLLYWOOD CASINO AT CHARLES TOWN RACING

Many enjoy the thrill of a horse race and several can be seen in Charles Town, West Virginia. The race track offers onsite betting and a casino for those who wish to tango with lady luck. A shuttle service will even take you back to the associated inn. If visiting, make sure to try one of several eateries that will give you a taste of home. This local loves to watch the horses enter the track as excitement builds. Take a chance on a horse that grabs your attention and cheer them on to the finish line.

14. BURNING ROCK OUTDOOR ADVENTURE PARK

Visiting West Virginia means spending time enjoying the great outdoors. One way to do this in a family friendly way is to visit Burning Rock Outdoor Adventure Park located just outside of Beckley. Over 100 miles of trails for anyone from novice to pro exist for every type of bike, ATV, or UTV. Camp on the grounds or rent a rustic cabin. The park is seasonal, but well worth the trip if you want a real adventure. Some weekends races are occurring and allow visitors to watch as competitors of all ages race to the finish line. Perfect for all ages and all levels as this adventure park offers a little something for everyone. If going to watch the races make a full day out of the event. All upcoming races and schedules can be found online.

15. ENJOY THE MOUNTAINS: SNOWSHOE MOUNTAIN RESORT

The mountains are the best part of wild, wonderful, West Virginia and Snowshoe will not disappoint. Whether you are like me and enjoy the winter snow on the slopes or want to hike, bike, and camp in the summer months, this resort has something for everyone. Rough it in a tent or rent a cabin or local room. Even after a hard day of outdoor play, the amazing views will make you want to relax and just enjoy the scenery. Slopes range in levels so be prepared for a challenge no matter your ability. Specific information and the number of open slopes are updated on the website to make sure you get the most out of your adventure.

>TOURIST

16. BABCOCK STATE PARK

One of this writer's favorite destinations, Babcock State Park not only offers amazing views, but has a working grist mill that has been the subject of many photos over the years. For a family centered adventure take a trail ride through the woods or ride down to the river and then raft back out. It will be an adventure you never forget. Trail rides can be scheduled in advance, but fair warning the terrain is safe but a little rough. Even large groups can schedule these horseback rides. If horses are not your thing then take a hike through the beautiful forests that are Babcock. Take a picnic lunch and sit by the gristmill to enjoy the sound of the water. If you enjoy geocaching then this activity is also offered with a list of caches on the park website, including those at other parks. If you wish to place a cache then an application is needed, but the form is easily downloaded online as well. Happy hunting.

17. WHITE WATER RAFTING IN NEW RIVER

While the mountains are the highlight of West Virginia going river rafting also offers amazing views and a wild adventure. Perfect as a family activity, book a guide and hop into a raft to hit the rapids. Children as young as six can join in the fun with overnight trips available in cabins or through other camping options. Spend the day rafting and the evening by a campfire roasting marshmallows. If you want to really challenge yourself, try the Cliffside zip line that will make you feel like you are flying. Several rafting companies exist, but Ace is the most family friendly. Make sure to check levels and age requirements before scheduling a trip as some of the rapids are much more challenging than the others. For those who are experienced, the rapids are better later in the year closer to the fall months.

18. SECRET SANDWICH SOCIETY

Everyone needs to have a good meal while visiting West Virginia and one of the most unique options is the Secret Sandwich Society in Fayetteville, West Virginia. A unique menu of burgers, sandwiches, soup, beer, and dessert, this quaint little restaurant is located on the side of a hill and is always hopping. Try a local beer, cider, or even wine and enjoy good conversation with patrons and staff alike.

>TOURIST

19. WEATHERED GROUND BREWERY

Recently opened, this locally owned brewery offers food, fun, and beer on tap for individuals, tours, and special events. While non-alcoholic beverages are available, if visiting you should give one of the ten on-tap beers a try. Weekends during the warmer months offer outdoor activities such as corn hole and live music. Plan a reunion, a quick snack, or a weekend with the family friendly events in this gorgeous barn style brewery located in Cool Ridge West Virginia.

20. TAMARACK: CRAFTS, FOOD, AND FUN

All of West Virginia offered under one roof can be found at Tamarack in Beckley, West Virginia. This uniquely shaped conference center is just above the travel plaza and offers a huge array of locally made crafts. Local artists often demonstrate their trade in Tamarack. If visiting make sure to check out all the crafts from coal statuettes to locally made wines, jams, and jellies. Stay to enjoy a meal created by chefs from the Greenbrier resort. Family friendly with a variety of items that will make you want to come back for more. Dining is available indoors or out in the center courtyard. This writer recommends the bar-b-cue, but the chicken, fish, and any dessert are also delicious.

21. WEST VIRGINIA STATE FAIR

A yearly favorite for locals from all over the state, the WV State Fair happens in early August. Basic carnival rides and games are typical, but the real fun is found in the variety of animals and shows that occur. One of the largest horse shows in the area happens throughout the week with horses of all styles and abilities. Additionally, 4-H competitors show every animal from sheep and cows to rabbits. Walk through the exhibits that showcase local talent and try the delicious food that cannot be beat. Concerts happen at least once a day and tickets are available online typically starting in mid-June. Take it from this local, try the enormous cinnamon rolls and the roasted corn on the cob for a real mountain state experience.

>TOURIST

22. VIA FERRATA

Not for the faint of heart, the Via Ferrata offers zip lines and a climb known as the Iron Way. The Iron Way is a three and a half to five hour climb that requires the crossing of a suspension bridge and fixed anchor climbing with a guide. Take in the views from over a thousand feet in the air with this breathtaking climb. This is definitely a challenge that should be undertaken by those in good shape. The climb is available year round if the weather permits.

23. WINTER FUN AT WINTERPLACE

The mountains of West Virginia are a great thing to enjoy in the summer, but if winter sports are more your style then Winterplace offers a family friendly destination. Take on a bunny slope or a black diamond trail in this winter destination located just off the interstate in Flat Top, West Virginia. If you do not want to ski, enjoy the tubing area where you can slide down an icy slope on a huge inner tube over and over again. Take a break in the cafeteria for hot chocolate and snacks or at the lodge for drinks and a meal. Ski rentals and lodging is available. Lessons are also available for those who may just be learning to ski at any age. A small area for kids only skiing is also available.

24. BRIDGE WALK

Though the New River Gorge Bridge is a site to behold, true thrill seekers will enjoy the bridge walk that allows you to get up close and personal with the structure of the bridge. The 900 foot walk across the canyon offers breath-taking views of the mountains and New River below. This is an experience that everyone should attempt at some point in their lives. Safety harnesses offer a bit of safety for all adventurers. This walk is actually under the bridge and is a little known attraction, but well worth the effort and scheduling.

25. SENECA ROCK

Test your strength and ability with wilderness climbing at Seneca Rock. A challenge to locals and visitors alike Seneca is a great climb in the summer, spring, and especially the autumn when the leaves are starting to change. There is a non-climber option with a 1.3 mile interpretive trail that offers the same scenic

>TOURIST

views with much less effort. This writer recommends a spring or fall visit, but all open seasons offer amazing views.

26. A TRUE TREE HOUSE: THORNY MOUNTAIN FIRE TOWER

If visiting the Greenbrier River Valley take time to sleep under the stars in a real fire tower that is 65 feet tall on top of a mountain peak. Just like sleeping in a fancier version of your childhood tree house, this fire tower allows you to feel like you are on top of the world in the Seneca State Forest. Hike, bike, and fish during the day and spend the night on a cot with 360 degree views in the fire tower. The tower can be booked between May and October. This overnight destination is not for the faint of heart as the tower truly towers above the ground.

27. SUMMERSVILLE LAKE

During the summer months (May to September), Summersville lake is a local favorite spot. This clear freshwater lake is perfect for swimming, boating, and water skiing. The best part is Sarge's Dive Shop that will teach and take you diving in the warm water to view local aquatic life close up. There are several diving spots available for all levels and a small sunken boat that can be explored if wanted. Great for some fun in the sun with amazing views both above and below the water. Take the time to go for a dive if possible, even as a local there is always something new to see or explore.

28. APPALACHIAN TRAIL

The great outdoors are meant to be enjoyed and one place to truly take in the beauty of West Virginia is the Appalachian Trail. Start your journey by crossing the footbridge at Harpers Ferry and continue on as far as you would like to go. The trail is very long and while only four miles are in West Virginia the hike is well worth the effort. This local recommends hiking in the summer if you want to see local wildlife or in the fall to enjoy the beauty of the changing leaves. If coming in the fall make sure to check the weather to bring appropriate gear. Some autumns are unseasonably warm while others bring on an early snow fall and freezing temperatures.

>TOURIST

29. LOST WORLD CAVERNS

West Virginia is known for the mountains which mean there are some amazing caves to explore. Lost World Caverns in Lewisburg, West Virginia offers a chance for explorers to view huge stalactites and stalagmites or spend time exploring wild caves in the area. Dress for being underground as the caves can get chilly, but the setting is magical and one that should not be missed. Growing up, this writer loved going to see the natural structures the caves offer. Be warned, at one time a supermarket tabloid claimed this to be home to the half bat/half boy called Batboy. This local will remind you to take a camera or your phone as the caverns offer great photo ops with amazing scenery that cannot be seen above ground.

30. GRANDVIEW OUTDOOR DRAMA

If visiting the area in the summer months make sure to stop by a local favorite activity, the Grandview Outdoor Drama. Located in Grandview State Park the amphitheater offers several shows a week during the summer months. A yearly favorite is the story of Hatfield's and McCoy's and the famous fight that ensued. Each year a new play or musical is added as an option for visitors and locals alike. I have seen numerous plays over the years and have a new appreciation for theater because of this outdoor drama. Be warned at since this is outdoors the weather can occasionally cancel plays. Also know that bats will fly around near the stage but are never a real problem for actors or patrons. Feel free to take a blanket to cuddle up in as the temperature dips a little in the evenings.

31. DOLLY SODS

As someone who grew up enjoying a camp out in the yard at different times during the summer months, Dolly Sods still offers views that are out of this world. Take time to camp under the stars that seem brighter than anywhere else in the state. Make sure to watch a sunrise before leaving to be reminded of the beautiful creation earth is in this galaxy. This area truly makes you feel like you are on top of the world. Take time to enjoy the simplicity of staring up at the stars and finding constellations, something that has often been forgotten in our technology focused world.

32. Cranberry Glades Botanical Area

>TOURIST

A highly unexpected area located in Richwood, West Virginia is the Cranberry Glade Botanical Area. The unique makeup of this boggy area allows plants, even carnivorous ones, to grow in the area. These plants are not typical of W.V. but are an amazing sight to behold. A large area can be explored by way of a footbridge that allows people to view without disturbing the plants. For locals, this is a way to see unique plant life without leaving the state. It is interesting to learn how such a place exists in the state of West Virginia.

33. SWISS VILLAGE

West Virginia may be known for many things, but one hidden local secret is the town of Helvetia in Randolph County. Nestled deep in the hills of W.V. and originally settled by the Swiss, this little area has maintained a large number of the Swiss traditions and food. Stop for a visit and enjoy a culinary journey that may seem a little out of place, but is well worth the journey. This local did not know that the Swiss had settled any part of West Virginia until stumbling upon this area during a road trip.

34. HARPERS FERRY

West Virginia has a rich history that can be found in nearly every county. From small towns to the larger cities there is a piece of history that can be found. Harpers Ferry is no exception. When John Brown raided Harpers Ferry the place became infamous. If you want to learn a little more about the raid in a unique way, visit the wax museum that shares further information. The wax figures are life size with close to 90 figures included. The wax figures can be a little off putting at first, but the history that comes to life is both fun and educational.

35. THE COAL HOUSE

West Virginia coal mines are on the news often, sometimes good and sometimes not great, but the fact remains that coal makes West Virginia come alive. We love coal so much that there is an entire house made of coal. Stop in and explore this unique creation in Mingo County. Locals appreciate the work that went into this structure and while others may wonder why such a building was made. Stop by and take a look yourself and make your own judgment.

>TOURIST

36. HILLBILLY HOTDOG

West Virginia has a great number of stereotypes and each is laughed at by locals. Stop by a very unique eatery in Lesage, West Virginia to have a little fun and some good food in this trailer park looking setting. The gourmet burgers and hot dogs are delicious. No worries, locals love the food and allow visitors to poke some fun at all everyone believes about the state. Grab a t-shirt, some photos, and even some hillbilly stemware (mason jars on stands) to add to your memoires of your W.V. adventure. Gifts are available online as well, but this is an experience that no one should miss when travelling through West Virginia. Ironically, the owners were not West Virginia natives but they have made themselves at home over the years and created a unique selection of gourmet hot dogs and hamburgers that will leave you feelings full and happy. What other state encourages you to enjoy the stereotypes that are somewhat based in reality?

37. ROAD KILL COOK OFF

If you are coming to West Virginia in the fall to check out the beautiful foliage, why not stop in

Pocahontas County for the Road Kill Cook Off. Don't let the name fool you, this place has some delicious treats, if you are brave enough to try the selection. Sample squirrel, bear, and deer specially prepared by entrants. Even the menus are written in 'hillbilly' with interesting spelling and special names like Bear Butt Stew or Busted Tailgate BBQ Mac and Cheese. This is an event that locals look forward to each year. Are you brave enough to try some specialty local cuisine? If so this is a one stop event to get the best of the best by locals.

38. BLACKWATER FALLS STATE PARK

The best thing about the West Virginia mountains is the unique landscapes that offer Mother Nature a chance to be amazing. Though there are numerous state parks in West Virginia the waterfalls in Blackwater Falls State Park are probably the most breathtaking. Several sets of falls exist and the river continues to rush for miles through the park. Flanked by gorgeous greenery the fallen red spruce needles and tannic acid from the plants is what give this water its unique color. This is a local favorite backdrop for photos. Visit one or all of the water falls in a single day or visit. Be ready to do a little light hiking to most of the destinations.

39. US CAPITOL BUILDING

Few states can boast about how recognizable their capitol building is against the backdrop of the town, but Charleston, WV offers a building that is instantly recognizable. Whether you simply want to learn about the history of the state or view this impressive gold coated dome, the capitol will meet those needs. This local went on numerous field trips to the capitol over the years and still remembers the tours that are currently offered daily. If you do not have time to stop for a tour at least take a few photos of the impressive dome as you drive by as the capitol is easily seen from the road.

40. WEST VIRGINIA STATE MUSEUM/CULTURAL CENTER

West Virginia is definitely rich in history in so many ways. One place to explore this history is at the Cultural Center in Charleston, West Virginia. Make it a day by also touring the capital. In the museum displays and explanations of the state's cultural, historical, art, and geological history are showcased. This local's favorite display is the reconstructed settler's cabin that is inside the museum. Spend a couple hours or an entire day. Many local eateries are nearby that will satisfy even the pickiest of eaters.

41. HERITAGE FARM MUSEUM AND VILLAGE

Located in Huntington, West Virginia this farm museum will take you back in time with handmade log cabins, a blacksmith shop, and even a children's machine discovery zone. Pulling onto the property allows visitors and locals alike to step back into a much simpler time. Aside from the museums that can be toured there are hiking trails, guided tours, crafts, and even a gift shop. Let your family experience what it is like to be a pioneer in a much simpler time. This local visits with family and enjoys the time cell phone free to see what life was like not that long ago.

42. GLADE SPRINGS RESORT

Glade Springs Resort is a visitors dream for family activities. Located just outside of Beckley, West Virginia, Glad Springs offers three championship golf course, stables for lessons or trail rides, carriage rides, and a spa. Stay at the Inn at the resort or for longer stays rent a chalet to feel more at home. If visiting in the winter there are shuttles to Winterplace Ski Resort that is nearby. This local recommends a trail ride through the woods and then a relaxing trip to the spa. The golf courses are challenging and beautifully manicured for even the most discerning golfer. The pro shop offers equipment and a place to dine after a long day on the greens. If planning an event there is a conference center on the grounds and reservations can be made for all activities ahead of time.

43. ADVENTURES ON THE GORGE

This central location for adventure is located in Lansing, West Virginia on the New River. This is truly a one stop shop for all your outdoor adventure needs. The best time to visit is just after labor day when the river is up and the best rafting adventures are offered, but even if you don't want to tackle the rapids there are opportunities for zip lining, canopy tours, rappelling, rock climbing, paint ball, and so much more. Rent a cabin and stay on the river or take an overnight camping trip in which you raft for the whole day. This local recommends rafting the lower New River for a challenge and a canopy tour for the adventurous. Zip lining through the hills is also a breathtaking adventure that allows for beautiful pictures; just make sure to hold tight to your phone or camera.

44. BLUEBERRY HILL

If you find yourself in West Virginia during blueberry season then stop by and pick some of your own at Blueberry Hill. Located in Flat Top, West Virginia this blueberry farm is a local favorite for finding the biggest, best blueberries around. They provide the buckets and you provide the picking power. No one minds if you taste a few while picking your fill to take home. Call ahead as the season varies, but the family owned farm is full of helpful people who will only offer you the best. The best time to visit is late July, but feel free to call ahead the numbers can be found online.

45. OKES FAMILY FARM

Okes Family Farm is a go to destination each year around Halloween. The large family run farm offers an enormous pick your own pumpkin patch each year that includes a corn maze and giant hay spider for great photo ops. Not only can you choose a pumpkin but often hay rides, face painting, and even a bounce house are available for a day filled with family fun. This local loves to go pick out a couple pumpkins for a yearly carving party to celebrate Halloween. Take time to visit with the owners or just enjoy some much needed fun with the family. Prices are reasonable and a whole day can be spent in the corn maze or picking out the perfect pumpkin.

46. CHARLESTON, WEST VIRGINIA

Though West Virginia is mostly about the wild, wonderful outdoor adventures, there are areas to step away from nature for a few days. Visit Charleston, WV to take in a concert or game, shop at the Capitol Market that offers seasonal produce and an indoor artisanal mall, or even head to Cato Park to swim. At the heart of Charleston is the Town Center Mall that is one of the largest east of the Mississippi. So if you are tired of the great outdoors or just need a break then head to Charleston and take a day to have a different type of fun. This local, even though she is an adult, still enjoys the Disney store and Build-A Bear at the mall. Such a variety of stores exist that the entire day can be spent shopping for anything you may need.

47. OUT OF THE BOX ROOM ESCAPE

Try out your survival and deduction skills in the Out of the Box Room Escape in Princeton, West Virginia. Though this creation is sometimes moved to new areas as a promotional game, finding the activity is well worth a bit of research. Go into the room and see what items you can find to escape before time runs out. Work your way through problems and challenge the mind with this thought provoking and fun activity for the whole family. This writer has been twice and it was different each time, I did beat the timer the second time, but not the first. So get your heart racing as you try to beat the clock with family or friends.

48. LAKE STEVENS

Lake Stevens is a local favorite for so many reasons. Whether you want to fish, lie in the sun, enjoy the simple water park, or enjoy a boat ride, this is a one stop shop. Even living locally we often rent a cabin for a week to fully enjoy the experience. There is even an area for paintball and horseback riding if water activities are not your style. Located in Beckley, Lake Stevens is a great place for family and friends. Make sure you pack your suit, towel, and sunscreen for a day, weekend, or week on the lake.

49. LEWISBURG CHOCOLATE FESTIVAL

If you have an insatiable sweet tooth then make a day trip to Lewisburg for the Chocolate Festival each April. The one day festival offers locals a chance to showcase their skills as visitors get to sample chocolate in all its forms. As you enter the festival area you even receive a menu of all the available items so you know where to start. If you find something you must have more of, take a selection home as vendors are also selling their wares. This local would not miss a festival ever and will always recommend the cookie shots that are often available. The best part is the smell of chocolate that seems to stick with you throughout the day.

50. HARVEST MOON AND CRAFTS FESTIVAL

West Virginia pride is truly showcased at the Harvest Moon and Crafts Festival in Parkersburg. Taking place in September, the two day event has over 200 crafters, tasty food, and live entertainment. Allow the true mountaineers to showcase their crafting ability while enjoying good music and mountain state treats. Crafts range from coal carvings to quilts and everything in between. Enjoy the country charm while conversing with locals from around the state. You can even leave with a few unique decorations that will remind you of your trip. A perfect weekend vacation for locals and visitors alike. If you have time stay for the PaddleFest and Downtown Throwdown BBQ for the best BBQ in the state.

>TOURIST

TOP REASONS TO BOOK THIS TRIP

Mountains – The mountains of West Virginia offer great views, awesome outdoor adventures, and scenery that is unmatched. Whether you want to experience snowcapped mountains, colorful autumn leaves, or fields full of wildflowers, this is the state to visit.

Food – Though West Virginia may not be gourmet, the down home country cooking you can get at many of the unique eateries will leave you wanting more. Don't get this writer wrong, gourmet food is available, but if visiting the state why not immerse yourself in the country culture that is part of the charm.

History – West Virginia is rich in history from Harpers Ferry battles to more recent coal camps. Come to explore the rich history of the Mountain state and learn more about this friendly, fun-filled area that may have you considering moving to make this home.

>TOURIST

BONUS BOOK

50 THINGS TO KNOW ABOUT PACKING LIGHT FOR TRAVEL

PACK THE RIGHT WAY EVERY TIME

AUTHOR: MANIDIPA BHATTACHARYYA

First Published in 2015 by Dr. Lisa Rusczyk. Copyright 2015. All Rights Reserved. No part of this publication may be reproduced, including scanning and photocopying, or distributed in any form or by any means, electronic or mechanical, or stored in a database or retrieval system without prior written permission from the publisher.

Disclaimer: The publisher has put forth an effort in preparing and arranging this book. The information provided herein by the author is provided "as is". Use this information at your own risk. The publisher is not a licensed doctor. Consult your doctor before engaging in any medical activities. The publisher and author disclaim any liabilities for any loss of profit or commercial or personal damages resulting from the information contained in this book.

Edited by Melanie Howthorne

ABOUT THE AUTHOR

Manidipa Bhattacharyya is a creative writer and editor, with an education in English literature and Linguistics. After working in the IT industry for seven long years she decided to call it quits and follow her heart instead. Manidipa has been ghost writing, editing, proof reading and doing secondary research services for many story tellers and article writers for about three years. She stays in Kolkata, India with her husband and a busy two year old. In her own time Manidipa enjoys travelling, photography and writing flash fiction.

Manidipa believes in travelling light and never carries anything that she couldn't haul herself on a trip. However, travelling with her child changed the scenario. She seemed to carry the entire world with her for the baby on the first two trips. But good sense prevailed and she is again working her way to becoming a light traveler, this time with a kid.

INTRODUCTION

*He who would travel happily
must travel light.*

-Antoine de Saint-Exupéry

Travel takes you to different places from seas and mountains to deserts and much more. In your travels you get to interact with different people and their cultures. You will, however, enjoy the sights and interact positively with these new people even more, if you are travelling light.

When you travel light your mind can be free from worry about your belongings. You do not have to spend precious vacation time waiting for your luggage to arrive after a long flight. There is be no chance of your bags going missing and the best part is that you need not pay a fee for checked baggage.

People who have mastered this art of packing light will root for you to take only one carry-on, wherever you go. However, many people can find it really hard to pack light. More so if you are travelling with children. Differentiating between "must have" and "just in case" items is the starting point. There will be ample shopping avenues at your destination which are just waiting to be explored.

This book will show you 'packing' in a new 'light' – pun intended – and help you to embrace light packing practices for all of your future travels.

Off to packing!

DEDICATION

I dedicate this book to all the travel buffs that I know, who have given me great insights into the contents of their backpacks.

THE RIGHT TRAVEL GEAR

1. CHOOSE YOUR TRAVEL GEAR CAREFULLY

While selecting your travel gear, pick items that are light weight, durable and most importantly, easy to carry. There are cases with wheels so you can drag them along – these are usually on the heavy side because of the trolley. Alternatively a backpack that you can carry comfortably on your back, or even a duffel bag that you can carry easily by hand or sling across your body are also great options. Whatever you choose, one thing to keep in mind is that the luggage itself should not weigh a ton, this will give you the flexibility to bring along one extra pair of shoes if you so desire.

2. CARRY THE MINIMUM NUMBER OF BAGS

Selecting light weight luggage is not everything. You need to restrict the number of bags you carry as well. One carry-on size bag is ideal for light travel. Most carriers allow one cabin baggage plus one purse, handbag or camera bag as long as it slides under the seat in front. So technically, you can carry two items of luggage without checking them in.

3. PACK ONE EXTRA BAG

Always pack one extra empty bag along with your essential items. This could be a very light weight duffel bag or even a sturdy tote bag which takes up minimal space. In the event that you end up buying a lot of souvenirs, you already have a handy bag to stuff all that into and do not have to spend time hunting for an appropriate bag.

I'm very strict with my packing and have everything in its right place. I never change a rule. I hardly use anything in the hotel room. I wheel my own wardrobe in and that's it.

Charlie Watts

CLOTHES & ACCESSORIES

4. PLAN AHEAD

Figure out in advance what you plan to do on your trip. That will help you to pick that one dress you need for the occasion. If you are going to attend a wedding then you have to carry formal wear. If not, you can ditch the gown for something lighter that will be comfortable during long walks or on the beach.

5. WEAR THAT JACKET

Remember that wearing items will not add extra luggage for your air travel. So wear that bulky jacket that you plan to carry for your trip. This saves space and can also help keep you warm during the chilly flight.

6. MIX AND MATCH

Carry clothes that can be interchangeably used to reinvent your look. Find one top that goes well with a couple of pairs of pants or skirts. Use tops, shirts and jackets wisely along with other accessories like a scarf or a stole to create a new look.

7. CHOOSE YOUR FABRIC WISELY

Stuffing clothes in cramped bags definitely takes its toll which results in wrinkles. It is best to carry wrinkle free, synthetic clothes or merino tops. This will eliminate the need for that small iron you usually bring along.

8. DITCH CLOTHES PACK UNDERWEAR

Pack more underwear and socks. These are the things that will give you a fresh feel even if you do not get a chance to wear fresh clothes. Moreover these are easy to wash and can be dried inside the hotel room itself.

9. CHOOSE DARK OVER LIGHT

While picking your clothes choose dark coloured ones. They are easy to colour coordinate and can last longer before needing a wash. Accidental food spills and dirt from the road are less visible on darker clothes.

10. WEAR YOUR JEANS

Take only one pair of Jeans with you, which you should wear on the flight. Remember to pick a pair that can be worn for sightseeing trips and is equally eloquent for dinner. You can add variety by adding light weight cargoes and chinos.

11. CARRY SMART ACCESSORIES

The right accessory can give you a fresh look even with the same old dress. An intelligent neck-piece, a couple of bright scarves, stoles or a sarong can be used in a number of ways to add variety to your clothing. These light weight beauties can double up as a nursing cover, a light blanket, beach wear, a modesty cover for visiting places of worship, and also makes for an enthralling game of peek-a-boo.

12. LEARN TO FOLD YOUR GARMENTS

Seasoned travellers all swear by rolling their clothes for compact and wrinkle free packing. Bundle packing, where you roll the clothes around a central object as if tying it up, is also a popular method of compact and wrinkle free packing. Stacking folded clothes one on top of another is a big no-no as it makes creases extreme and they are difficult to get rid of without ironing.

13. WASH YOUR DIRTY LAUNDRY

One of the ways to avoid carrying loads of clothes is to wash the clothes you carry. At some places you might get to use the laundry services or a Laundromat but if you are in a pinch, best solution is to wash them yourself. If that is the plan then carrying quick drying clothes is highly recommended, which most often also happen to be the wrinkle free variety.

14. LEAVE THOSE TOWELS BEHIND

Regular towels take up a lot of space, are heavy and take ages to dry out. If you are staying at hotels they will provide you with towels anyway. If you are travelling to a remote place, where the availability of towels look doubtful, carry a light weight travel towel of viscose material to do the job.

15. USE A COMPRESSION BAG

Compression bags are getting lots of recommendation now days from regular travellers. These are useful for saving space in your luggage when you have to pack bulky dresses. While packing for the return trip, get help from the hotel staff to arrange a vacuum cleaner.

FOOTWEAR

16. PUT ON YOUR HIKING BOOTS

If you have plans to go hiking or trekking during your trip, you will need those bulky hiking boots. The best way to carry them is to wear them on flight to save space and luggage weight. You can remove the boots once inside and be comfortable in your socks.

17. PICKING THE RIGHT SHOES

Shoes are often the bulkiest items, along with being the dainty if you are a female. They need care and take up a lot of space in your luggage. It is advisable therefore to pick shoes very carefully. If you plan to do a lot of walking and site seeing, then wearing a pair of comfortable walking shoes are a must. For more formal occasions you can carry durable, light weight flats which will not take up much space.

18. STUFF SHOES

If you happen to pack a pair of shoes, ensure you utilize their hollow insides. Tuck small items like rolled up socks or belts to save space. They will also be easy to find.

> TOURIST

TOILETRIES

19. STASHING TOILETRIES

Carry only absolute necessities. Airline rules dictate that for one carry-on bag, liquids and gels must be in 3.4 ounce (100ml) bottles or less, and must be packed in a one quart zip-lock bag. If you are planning to stay in a hotel, the basic things will be provided for you. It's best is to buy the rest from the local market at your destination.

20. TAKE ALONG TAMPONS

Tampons are a hard to find item in a lot of countries. Figure out how many you need and pack accordingly. For longer stays you can buy them online and have them delivered to where you are staying.

21. GET PAMPERED BEFORE YOU TRAVEL

Some avid travellers suggest getting a pedicure and manicure just the day before travelling. This not only gives you a well kept look, you also save the trouble of packing nail polish. Remember, every little bit of weight reduced adds up.

ELECTRONICS
22. LUGGING ALONG ELECTRONICS

Electronics have a large role to play in our lives today. Most of us cannot imagine our lives away from our phones, laptops or tablets. However while travelling, one must consider the amount of weight these electronics add to our luggage. Thankfully smart phones come along with all the essentials tools like a camera, email access, picture editing tools and more. They are smart to the point of eliminating the need to carry multiple gadgets. Choose a smart phone that suits all your requirements and travel with the world in your palms or pocket.

23. REDUCE THE NUMBER OF CHARGERS

If you do travel with multiple electronic devices, you will have to bear the additional burden of carrying all their chargers too. Check if a single charger can be used for multiple devices. You might also consider investing in a pocket charger. These small devices support multiple devices while keeping you charged on the go.

24. TRAVEL FRIENDLY APPS

Along with smart phones come numerous apps, which are immensely helpful in our travels. You name it and you have an app for it at hand – take pictures, sharing with friends and family, torch to light dark roads, maps, checking flight/train times, find hotels and many other things. Use these smart alternatives to traditional items like books to eliminate weight and save space.

*I get ideas about what's essential
when packing my suitcase.*

-Diane von Furstenberg

TRAVELLING WITH KIDS

25. BRING ALONG THE STROLLER

Kids might enjoy walking for a while but they soon tire out and a stroller is the just the right thing for them to rest in while you continue your tour. Strollers also double duty as a luggage carrier and shopping bag holder. Remember to pick a light weight, easy to handle brand of stroller. Better yet, find out in advance if you can rent a stroller at your destination.

26. BRING ONLY ENOUGH DIAPERS FOR YOUR TRIP

Diapers take up a lot of space and add to the weight of your luggage. Therefore it is advisable to carry just enough diapers to last through the trip and a few for afterwards, till you buy fresh stock at your destination. Unless of course you are travelling to a really remote area, in which case you have no choice but to carry the load. Otherwise diapers are something you will find pretty easily.

27. TAKE ONLY A COUPLE OF TOYS

Children are easily attracted by new things in their environment. While travelling they will find numerous 'new' objects to scrutinize and play with. Packing just one favorite toy is enough, or if there is no favorite toy leave out all of them in favor of stories or imaginary games.

28. CARRY KID FRIENDLY SNACKS

Create a small snack counter in your bag to store away quick bites for those sudden hunger pangs. Depending on the child's age this could include chocolates, raisins, dry fruits, granola bars or biscuits. Also keep a bottle of water handy for your little one. These things do not add much weight and can be adjusted in a handbag or knapsack.

29. GAMES TO CARRY

Create some travel specific, imaginary games if you have slightly grown up children, like spot the attractions. Keep a coloring book and colors handy for in-flight or hotel time. Apps on your smart phone can keep the children engaged with cartoons and story books. Older children are often entertained by games available on phones or tablets. This cuts the weight of luggage down while keeping the kids entertained.

30. LET THE KIDS CARRY THEIR LOAD

A good thing is to start early sharing of responsibilities. Let your child pick a bag of his or her choice and pack it themselves. Keep tabs on what they are stuffing in their bags by asking if they will be using that item on the trip. It could start out being just an entertainment bag initially but with growing years they will learn to sort the useful from the superfluous. Children as little as four can maneuver a small trolley suitcase like a pro- their experience in pull along toys credit. If you are worried that you may be pulling it for them, you may want to start with a backpack.

31. DECIDE ON LOCATION FOR CHILDREN TO SLEEP

While on a trip you might not always get a crib at your destination, and carrying one will make life all the more difficult. Instead call ahead to see if there are any cribs or roll out beds for children. You may even put blankets on the floor. Weave them a story about camping and they will gladly sleep without any trouble.

32. GET BABY PRODUCTS DELIVERED AT YOUR DESTINATION

If you are absolutely paranoid about not getting your favourite variety of diaper or brand of baby food, check out online stores like amazon.com for services in your destination city. You can buy things online ahead of your travel and get them delivered to your hotel upon arrival.

33. FEEDING NEEDS OF YOUR INFANTS

If you are travelling with a breastfed infant, you save the trouble of carrying bottles and bottle sanitization kits. For special food, or medications, you may need to call ahead to make sure you have a refrigerator where you are staying.

34. FEEDING NEEDS OF YOUR TODDLER

With the progression from infancy to toddler, their dietary requirements too evolve. You will have to pack some snacks for travelling time. Fresh fruits and vegetables can be purchased at your destination. Most of the cities you travel to in whichever part of the world, will have baby food products and formulas, available at the local drug-store or the supermarket.

35. PICKING CLOTHES FOR YOUR BABY

Contrary to popular belief, babies can do without many changes of clothes. At the most pack 2 outfits per day. Pack mix and match type clothes for your little one as well. Pick things which are comfortable to wear and quick to dry.

36. SELECTING SHOES FOR YOUR BABY

Like outfits, kids can make do with two pairs of comfortable shoes. If you can get some water resistant shoes it will be best. To expedite drying wet shoes, you can stuff newspaper in them then wrap them with newspaper and leave them to dry overnight.

37. KEEP ONE CHANGE OF CLOTHES HANDY

Travelling with kids can be tricky. Keep a change of clothes for the kids and mum handy in your purse or tote bag. This takes a bit of space in your hand luggage but comes extremely handy in case there are any accidents or spills.

38. LEAVE BEHIND BABY ACCESSORIES

Baby accessories like their bed, bath tub, car seat, crib etc. should be left at home. Many hotels provide a crib on request, while car seats can be borrowed from friends or rented. Babies can be given a bath in the hotel sink or even in the adult bath tub with a little bit of water. If you bring a few bath toys, they can be used in the bath, pool, and out of water. They can also be sanitized easily in the sink.

39. CARRY A SMALL LOAD OF PLASTIC BAGS

With children around there are chances of a number of soiled clothes and diapers. These plastic bags help to sort the dirt from the clean inside your big bag. These are very light weight and come in handy to other carry stuff as well at times.

PACK WITH A PURPOSE

40. PACKING FOR BUSINESS TRIPS

One neutral-colored suit should suffice. It can be paired with different shirts, ties and accessories for different occasions. One pair of black suit pants could be worn with a matching jacket for the office or with a snazzy top for dinner.

41. PACKING FOR A CRUISE

Most cruises have formal dinners, and that formal dress usually takes up a lot of space. However you might find a tuxedo to rent. For women, a short black dress with multiple accessory options will do the trick.

42. PACKING FOR A LONG TRIP OVER DIFFERENT CLIMATES

The secret packing mantra for travel over multiple climates is layering. Layering traps air around your body creating insulation against the cold. The same light t-shirt that is comfortable in a warmer climate can be the innermost layer in a colder climate.

REDUCE SOME MORE WEIGHT

43. LEAVE PRECIOUS THINGS AT HOME

Things that you would hate to lose or get damaged leave them at home. Precious jewelry, expensive gadgets or dresses, could be anything. You will not require these on your trip. Leave them at home and spare the load on your mind.

44. SEND SOUVENIRS BY MAIL

If you have spent all your money on purchasing souvenirs, carrying them back in the same bag that you brought along would be difficult. Either pack everything in another bag and check it in the airport or get everything shipped to your home. Use an international carrier for a secure transit, but this could be more expensive than the checking fees at the airport.

45. AVOID CARRYING BOOKS

Books equal to weight. There are many reading apps which you can download on your smart phone or tab. Plus there are gadgets like Kindle and Nook that are thinner and lighter alternatives to your regular book.

>TOURIST

CHECK, GET, SET, CHECK AGAIN

46. STRATEGIZE BEFORE PACKING

Create a travel list and prepare all that you think you need to carry along. Keep everything on your bed or floor before packing and then think through once again – do I really need that? Any item that meets this question can be avoided. Remove whatever you don't really need and pack the rest.

47. TEST YOUR LUGGAGE

Once you have fully packed for the trip take a test trip with your luggage. Take your bags and go to town for window shopping for an hour. If you enjoy your hour long trip it is good to go, if not, go home and reduce the load some more. Repeat this test till you hit the right weight.

48. ADD A ROLL OF DUCT TAPE

You might wonder why, when this book has been talking about reducing stuff, we're suddenly asking you to pack something totally unusual. This is because when you have limited supplies, duct tape is immensely helpful for small repairs – a broken bag, leaking zip-lock bag, broken sunglasses, you name it and duct tape can fix it, temporarily.

49. LIST OF ESSENTIAL ITEMS

Even though the emphasis is on packing light, there are things which have to be carried for any trip. Here is our list of essentials:

- Passport/Visa or any other ID
- Any other paper work that might be required on a trip like permits, hotel reservation confirmations etc.
- Medicines – all your prescription medicines and emergency kit, especially if you are travelling with children
- Medical or vaccination records
- Money in foreign currency if travelling to a different country
- Tickets- Email or Message them to your phone

50. MAKE THE MOST OF YOUR TRIP

Wherever you are going, whatever you hope to do we encourage you to embrace it whole-heartedly. Take in the scenery, the culture and above all, enjoy your time away from home.

On a long journey even a straw weighs heavy.

-Spanish Proverb

>TOURIST

PACKING AND PLANNING TIPS

A Week before Leaving

- Arrange for someone to take care of pets and water plants
- Stop mail and newspaper
- Notify Credit Card companies where you are going.
- Change your thermostat settings
- Car inspected, oil is changed, and tires have the correct pressure.
- Passports and id is up to date.
- Pay bills.
- Copy important items and download travel Apps.
- Start collecting small bills for tips

Right Before Leaving

- Clean out refrigerator.
- Empty garbage cans.
- Lock windows.
- Make sure you have the right ID with you.
- Bring cash for tips.
- Remember travel documents.
- Lock door behind you.
- Remember wallet.
- Unplug items in house and pack chargers.

>TOURIST

READ OTHER GREATER THAN A TOURIST BOOKS

Greater Than a Tourist San Miguel de Allende Guanajuato Mexico: 50 Travel Tips from a Local by Tom Peterson

Greater Than a Tourist – Lake George Area New York USA: 50 Travel Tips from a Local by Janine Hirschklau

Greater Than a Tourist – Monterey California United States: 50 Travel Tips from a Local by Katie Begley

Greater Than a Tourist – Chanai Crete Greece: 50 Travel Tips from a Local by Dimitra Papagrigoraki

Greater Than a Tourist – The Garden Route Western Cape Province South Africa: 50 Travel Tips from a Local by Li-Anne McGregor van Aardt

Greater Than a Tourist – Sevilla Andalusia Spain: 50 Travel Tips from a Local by Gabi Gazon

Greater Than a Tourist – Kota Bharu Kelantan Malaysia: 50 Travel Tips from a Local by Aditi Shukla

Children's Book: Charlie the Cavalier Travels the World by Lisa Rusczyk

> TOURIST

Visit Greater Than a Tourist for Free Travel Tips
http://GreaterThanATourist.com

Sign up for the Greater Than a Tourist Newsletter for discount days, new books, and travel information:
http://eepurl.com/cxspyf

Follow us on Facebook for tips, images, and ideas:
https://www.facebook.com/GreaterThanATourist

Follow us on Pinterest for travel tips and ideas:
http://pinterest.com/GreaterThanATourist

Follow us on Instagram for beautiful travel images:
http://Instagram.com/GreaterThanATourist

> TOURIST

Please leave your honest review of this book on Amazon and Goodreads. Please send your feedback to GreaterThanaTourist@gmail.com as we continue to improve the series. Thank you. We appreciate your positive and constructive feedback. Thank you.

>TOURIST

METRIC CONVERSIONS

TEMPERATURE

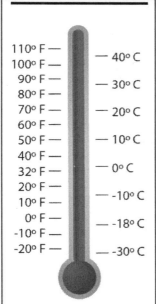

110° F — 40° C
100° F
90° F — 30° C
80° F
70° F — 20° C
60° F
50° F — 10° C
40° F
32° F — 0° C
20° F
10° F — -10° C
0° F
-10° F — -18° C
-20° F — -30° C

To convert F to C:
Subtract 32, and then multiply by 5/9 or .5555.

To Convert C to F:
Multiply by 1.8 and then add 32.

32F = 0C

LIQUID VOLUME

To Convert:................Multiply by
U.S. Gallons to Liters................. 3.8
U.S. Liters to Gallons 26
Imperial Gallons to U.S. Gallons 1.2
Imperial Gallons to Liters....... 4.55
Liters to Imperial Gallons 22
1 Liter = .26 U.S. Gallon
1 U.S. Gallon = 3.8 Liters

DISTANCE

To convert ....Multiply by
Inches to Centimeters 2.54
Centimeters to Inches 39
Feet to Meters....................... .3
Meters to Feet 3.28
Yards to Meters 91
Meters to Yards 1.09
Miles to Kilometers 1.61
Kilometers to Miles............ .62
1 Mile = 1.6 km
1 km = .62 Miles

WEIGHT

1 Ounce = .28 Grams
1 Pound = .4555 Kilograms
1 Gram = .04 Ounce
1 Kilogram = 2.2 Pounds

>TOURIST

TRAVEL QUESTIONS

- Do you bring presents home to family or friends after a vacation?
- Do you get motion sick?
- Do you have a favorite billboard?
- Do you know what to do if there is a flat tire?
- Do you like a sun roof open?
- Do you like to eat in the car?
- Do you like to wear sun glasses in the car?
- Do you like toppings on your ice cream?
- Do you use public bathrooms?
- Did you bring your cell phone and does it have power?
- Do you have a form of identification with you?
- Have you ever been pulled over by a cop?
- Have you ever given money to a stranger on a road trip?
- Have you ever taken a road trip with animals?
- Have you ever went on a vacation alone?
- Have you ever run out of gas?

- If you could move to any place in the world, where would it be?
- If you could travel anywhere in the world, where would you travel?
- If you could travel in any vehicle, which one would it be?
- If you had three things to wish for from a magic genie, what would they be?
- If you have a driver's license, how many times did it take you to pass the test?
- What are you the most afraid of on vacation?
- What do you want to get away from the most when you are on vacation?
- What foods smells bad to you?
- What item to you bring on ever trip with you away from home?
- What makes you sleepy?
- What song would you love to hear on the radio when you're cruising on the highway?
- What travel job would you want the least?
- What will you miss most while you are away from home?
- What is something you always wanted to try?

>TOURIST

- What is the best road side attraction that you ever saw?
- What is the farthest distance you ever biked?
- What is the farthest distance you ever walked?
- What is the weirdest thing you needed to buy while on vacation?
- What is your favorite candy?
- What is your favorite color car?
- What is your favorite family vacation?
- What is your favorite food in the world?
- What is your favorite gas station drink or food?
- What is your favorite license plate design?
- What is your favorite restaurant in the world?
- What is your favorite smell?
- What is your favorite song?
- What is your favorite sound that nature makes?
- What is your favorite thing to bring home from a vacation?
- What is your favorite vacation with friends?
- What is your favorite way to relax?

- What is your favorite weather conditions while driving?
- Where in the world would you rather never get to travel?
- Where is the farthest place you ever traveled in a car?
- Where is the farthest place you ever went North, South, East and West?
- Where is your favorite place in the world?
- Who is your favorite singer?
- Who taught you how to drive?
- Who will you miss the most while you are away?
- Who if the first person you will call when you get to your destination?
- Who brought you on your first vacation?
- Who likes to travel the most in your life?
- Would you rather be hot or cold?
- Would you rather drive above, below, or at the speed limited?
- Would you rather drive on a highway or a back road?
- Would you rather go on a train or a boat?
- Would you rather go to the beach or the woods?

\>TOURIST
TRAVEL BUCKET LIST

>TOURIST

NOTES

Made in the USA
Monee, IL
15 May 2020